Food Dudes

THE SMUCKER FAMILY

Jelly Pioneers

Heather C. Hudak

Checkerboard
Library

An Imprint of Abdo Publishing
www.abdopublishing.com

abdopublishing.com

Published by Abdo Publishing, a division of ABDO, PO Box 398166, Minneapolis, Minnesota 55439. Copyright © 2018 by Abdo Consulting Group, Inc. International copyrights reserved in all countries. No part of this book may be reproduced in any form without written permission from the publisher. Checkerboard Library™ is a trademark and logo of Abdo Publishing.

Printed in the United States of America, North Mankato, Minnesota
062017
092017

THIS BOOK CONTAINS RECYCLED MATERIALS

Production: Mighty Media, Inc.
Editor: Rebecca Felix
Cover Photographs: AP Images (inset), Shutterstock (main)
Interior Photographs: Alamy, pp. 7, 23; AP Images, pp. 21, 27; Courtesy Betsy Butler, p. 15; Eddie~S/Flickr, p. 11; iStockphoto, p. 13; Shutterstock, pp. 5, 6, 9, 12, 25; Wikimedia Commons, p. 24; Wisconsin Historical Society, WHS-66154, p. 17; Wisconsin Historical Society, WHS-66160, p. 19

Publisher's Cataloging-in-Publication Data

Names: Hudak, Heather C., 1975-, author.
Title: The Smucker family: jelly pioneers / by Heather C. Hudak.
Other titles: Jelly pioneers
Description: Minneapolis, MN : Abdo Publishing, 2018. | Series: Food dudes |
    Includes bibliographical references and index.
Identifiers: LCCN 2016962505 | ISBN 9781532110856 (lib. bdg.) |
    ISBN 9781680788709 (ebook)
Subjects: LCSH: Smucker, Jerome Monroe, 1858-1948--Juvenile literature. | J. M.
    Smucker Company (Firm)--United States--Biography--Juvenile literature. |
    Businesspeople--United States--Biography--Juvenile literature.
Classification: DDC 641.6 [B]--dc23
LC record available at http://lccn.loc.gov/2016962505

Contents

Jelly Giants

What is your favorite kind of sandwich? If you said peanut butter and jelly, you are not alone. In fact, it is one of the top ten favorite sandwiches in the United States. The next time you make a PB&J sandwich, take a close look at the labels on the jars. There is a good chance you will see "Smucker's" displayed in big, bold letters.

For more than 100 years, the Smucker family has been making some of the country's most popular jams, jellies, and spreads. Today, the Smucker name is on all types of products, including coffee, peanut butter, and chocolate syrup.

Smucker's was not always the massive company that it is now. It began with one man, J.M. Smucker. He sold apple butter out of the back of a wagon in the 1800s.

Jerome Monroe Smoker was born on December 5, 1858, in Orrville, Ohio. His parents, Gideon and Martha Magdalena, were **Mennonite** farmers. Jerome was the oldest of eight children. He had three sisters and four brothers.

Jerome's ancestor Christian Schmucker came to the United States from Switzerland in 1752. Years later, Christian's great-grandson, David, changed the family name to Smoker. He thought it sounded more American. David had nine children. Jerome's father, Gideon, was one of them. When he was an adult, Jerome changed the family name from Smoker to Smucker because he did not approve of smoking.

The Smucker's website shares fun recipes and tips for making PB&J sandwiches.

Family Farms

Jerome grew up farming his family's land. He later took a two-year program studying business at a local school. When he was done, he used what he learned about business to manage the farm. Eventually, the family business grew into four farms and a **creamery**.

In 1890, Smucker married Ella M. Yoder. The couple's oldest child, Willard, was born the following year. Twin sons, Willis and Wallace, were born in 1892, but they died the same year. Smucker and Ella's first daughter, Winna, was born in 1894.

By this time, the family farms were flourishing. Smucker had earned enough money to grow his business. He built a cider mill in 1897. At the mill, he made apple cider out of apples from a nearby orchard. The orchard was planted by John Chapman in the early 1800s. Chapman became known as Johnny Appleseed. He was famous for planting apple trees.

Today, the Smucker land in Orrville is home to a company visitor center and gift shop.

Smucker's businesses continued to grow. In 1899, his family did too. Another daughter, Wilma, was born that year. Smucker and Ella's youngest son, Welker, was born in 1906.

Apple Butter

Smucker's apple cider business was booming, but there was just one problem. Apples were only in season for part of the year in Ohio. Smucker needed to find a product to sell in the off-season. He began making apple butter using an old family recipe.

Fresh apples picked in fall spoiled by winter. So, people often turned the fruit into applesauce or apple butter to use over the winter months. These products did not spoil easily and would last a long time. Smucker used a special method for making his apple butter. It had a **unique** flavor that people enjoyed.

Smucker began selling his apple butter packaged in stoneware **crocks**. He was so proud of the quality of his products that he signed his name on the lid of each crock. Soon, the apple butter was even more popular than Smucker's other farm products.

By 10 years old, Smucker's oldest son, Willard, was helping with his father's business. He would load up a horse-drawn wagon with crocks of apple butter. Each crock held 0.5 gallons (2.27 L) and sold for 25 cents. Smucker and Willard traveled together across northeastern Ohio selling their apple butter.

Apple butter is made by slowly cooking apples with cider or water. This causes the apples' sugar to caramelize and turn brown.

Making It Official

Smucker fruit products quickly earned a reputation for quality. At the time, companies did not have to list ingredients on their labels. But Smucker did so anyway. He was happy to let his customers know what he was putting into each one of his products.

By 1915, Smucker was earning $60,000 per year in sales. That number more than doubled over the next few years. Finally in 1921, Smucker filed the paperwork to make his business official. He named it J.M. Smucker Company. Smucker owned 94 percent of the company. His children shared the remaining 6 percent.

Over the next two years, Smucker expanded the company's product line. In addition to apple butter, it made many flavors of jams and jellies. They were made from whole fruits or large fruit chunks and strained fruit juice. These products helped the company grow and became popular with customers.

J.M. Smucker Company soon came to be most often referred to as Smucker's. By the late 1920s, Smucker's was thriving. It had customers all over Ohio, Indiana, and Pennsylvania.

Although still officially the J.M. Smucker Company, the family uses "Smucker's" on all products, signs, and advertisements.

At the time, trains were the best way to ship products across these states. Smucker's was shipping so many products that the Pennsylvania Railroad built a track alongside the Smucker plant. This made pickups easier. Business was good for the Smucker family. But the 1930s brought unfortunate change.

Produce & Plants

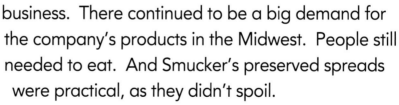

On October 29, 1929, life for most Americans took a turn for the worse. The **stock markets** crashed and investors lost a lot of money. This was the beginning of the **Great Depression**. It would affect the US **economy** for the next ten years.

At first, Smucker's continued to flourish even in the failing economy. For the first two years, its sales actually continued to rise. But by 1932, the company felt the Depression's effects. It lost money that year, as well as the next year.

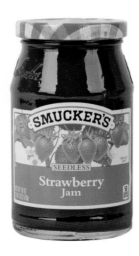

However, even in the poor economy, Smucker's stayed in business. There continued to be a big demand for the company's products in the Midwest. People still needed to eat. And Smucker's preserved spreads were practical, as they didn't spoil.

As the company stayed busy, Smucker began to hand over many responsibilities to Willard. In 1935, Willard **supervised** the opening of Smucker's first plant outside of Ohio. The fruit-processing facility was located in Washington State.

Washington was one of the country's top apple producers, making it the perfect place for the Smucker's plant. Apples were processed on site and then sent to the Orrville plant for cooking. With increased production, Smucker's was on its way to becoming a household name across the country.

Each Washington apple Smucker's uses in its spreads is picked by hand.

A New Look

Smucker's spreads continued to gain popularity in the coming years. But the large **crocks** were heavy and expensive to ship. In 1938, Willard decided it was time for a change. He designed a lightweight glass jar with a picture of a pioneer woman boiling apple butter.

People loved the new look. The company won an award at the National Packaging Show for best packaging design success. Sales soared over $1 million in 1939.

By this time, a third generation of Smuckers had joined the family business. After graduating from university in 1939, Willard's son Paul took a job at the Smucker company as an accountant. Paul took a short break from working at the Smucker company to serve in the US Navy during **World War II**. Three years later, he returned to Smucker's in a management position.

By 1942, Smucker products were being sold across the United States. But times were tough for the company during the war. Many men had been **drafted** to fight in the war, so it was hard to find workers to create the products. Many goods were also **rationed**

The winning 1938 apple butter label design shows a woman making apple butter over an open fire.

during the war, sent overseas to soldiers fighting. There were shortages on glass and fruit. Despite these challenges, Smucker's stayed afloat.

Quality Approved

Many companies struggled with ingredient or material shortages during the war. Some business owners did the best they could with lower-quality ingredients. They wanted to keep prices low for customers. But for the Smucker family, it was important to still give people a top-quality product at a price they could afford.

Other companies bought their fruits from markets. But the Smuckers went straight to local fruit farmers. Without a **middleman**, they could get better prices and pass the savings on to their customers. They could also control the quality of the fruits being used to make their jams and jellies.

The Smuckers were truly proud of their products. In 1946, they put their products' quality to the test. The company paid US government inspectors to review their production processes.

Smucker's was given the highest quality rating. This meant they could get a better price for their products. The government quality rating also prompted store owners to give Smucker's products the best spots on supermarket shelves. Better placement meant more people would see and buy their products.

QUALITY CONTROL
DEPARTMENT
INSPECTION RESPONSIBILITY
GLASS & CLOSURE
INGREDIENTS
FRUITS
FINISHED PRODUCTS

Smucker's inspects every material used in its production. This includes the glass and lids for the product containers.

In 1947, Smucker company celebrated its fiftieth anniversary. That same year, Willard took on the role of president of the company. But not long after, the family suffered a major loss. Smucker died in 1948 at 89 years old. It was up to Willard and Paul to carry on his **legacy**. They quickly went to work making a plan for the company's future success.

New Generation

In the 1950s, Paul continued to work alongside his father to make important decisions about the company. He continued to take on more and more responsibility. By 1954, Paul was the company's executive vice president.

Over the years, many well-known companies were interested in buying and taking over the successful Smucker company. This included food corporations Quaker Oats Company, Beatrice Foods, and Ralston Purina Company. But the Smuckers wanted to keep the business in the family.

In the late 1950s, however, the Smuckers decided to sell **shares** in their company. The Smucker family kept enough shares to maintain control of the business. They invested the money they earned from the sale back into the business.

Paul kept moving forward with plans to expand Smucker company. He started by opening a new plant in Salinas, California, in 1960. The new plant increased the Smucker company's ability to make products by more than 40 percent. But Paul was just getting started.

A Smucker's employee labels dozens of jelly jars. By the 1960s, the company's jams and jellies had become more popular than its apple butter.

Ads & Partners

Paul soon began buying other companies. He bought a jam and jelly company called Mary Ellen's, Inc. He also bought the H.B. DeViney Company, Inc., which was known for its peanut butter.

Owning new companies allowed Smucker's to start offering new products. This included ice cream toppings, syrups, and more. What was once a small-town apple butter business was now a major manufacturer of more than 100 food products.

The company continued to grow and change. In 1961, Paul took over the role of Smucker company president. In his new role, he had even bigger plans for the company. That year, he decided to place ads on the radio. He began working with an advertising agency to come up with something catchy.

In 1962, Smucker's unveiled its new **slogan**, "With a name like Smucker's, it has to be good." It was a huge success. Sales soared, doubling in just four years.

Despite this boost, Smucker's was still only the number two brand in the country. The company increased its **marketing** efforts. It put ads on television in a push for the top spot.

Smucker company expanded its products to include ketchup in 1963. Soon after, it made a deal with large food manufacturer Kellogg Company. The company would use Smucker's jam in its famous breakfast pastry Pop-Tarts.

By 1965, Smucker's began making its own line of peanut butter. But perhaps one of Smucker's most **unique** ideas was Goober. This combination of peanut butter and jelly in one jar was introduced in 1968. Despite its many new products, Smucker's jams, jellies, and preserves remained important products in the company.

Goober is available in grape or strawberry. These flavors are combined with stripes of peanut butter.

Basic Beliefs

Smucker's had seen more than fifty years of success. Much of this success was due to five beliefs Jerome Smucker **instilled** in the family business. The first was quality, which was considered most important in all aspects of the company.

Treating people well and fairly is also important at Smucker's. Following the company's **ethics** and looking for new ways to grow were the next two beliefs. Acting independently is the final one.

These beliefs had long been a part of the Smucker's business. In the late 1960s, Paul finally put the company's Basic Beliefs in writing. When his sons, Timothy and Richard, joined Smucker's in the 1970s, they used the Basic Beliefs to guide their future plans.

The 1970s were a trying time for Smucker's. The cost of making its products rose higher and higher. Profits dropped as a result. The company could have made some changes to the products so they would be cheaper to produce. But quality might have suffered. Smucker's refused to take that risk.

Timothy and Richard had a new vision for Smucker's. As vice president of planning, Timothy decided to modernize the

PLUMS

PEACHES

APPLES

APRICOTS

CHERRIES

Timothy (left) and Richard (right) worked very well together.
The brothers shared leadership of Smucker's for many years.

Basic Beliefs. He then included them in his business plan. With his brother's help, he was going to make Smucker's the number one brand in the United States.

Expanding Market

Smucker's Canadian headquarters in Ontario. The company began offering products in Canada in 1988.

Smucker's finally reached its goal in 1980. It was the number one brand of jelly and jams in the US market. The company had launched several new products in the mid-1970s, which had become very popular. They included a lower-priced line of jams and jellies, low-calorie and all-natural products, and a line of products aimed at kids. Smucker's also put more products on shelves and spent more on advertising.

In 1981, Timothy took over the role of president. Richard became the executive vice president. The brothers began buying other food companies and adding more products to the Smucker's label. These included Magic Shell ice cream toppings and Knudsen & Sons, Inc. pure fruit juices.

In the late 1980s, the Smuckers expanded the family business outside the United States. Smucker's products were now sold across the border in Canada. They also made their way to Australian grocery shelves. The company was officially international.

In 1987, Richard stepped into the role of president, and Timothy took over for his father as company chairman. Over the next **decade**, Timothy and Richard bought more food companies across the United States and in other parts of the world. In 1998, their father, Paul, died.

Smucker's Today

In 2004, *FORTUNE* magazine named Smucker's the best place to work in the United States. Each person hired to work at the company is considered part of the family. And each new employee receives a copy of a letter Paul wrote in the 1980s. It urges the employee to be kind to others and to have fun on the job.

Smucker's family values extend to its advertising too. The company will only advertise during family friendly television shows. And it pays US news program *TODAY* to air special announcements for people who are celebrating their one hundredth birthdays. The Smucker company wants its customers to know it cares about them and their families.

Throughout the 2000s, Smucker's bought some of the best-known brands in the food business. These included Crisco shortening, Pillsbury dough, and Folgers coffee. Smucker's also bought Jif peanut butter. It has been the leading peanut butter brand in the United States since 1981.

The Smucker's company also continued to come up with new products. Uncrustables were introduced in 1998. These are

Uncrustables have been a favorite in school lunches since their invention.

premade peanut butter and jelly sandwiches with their crusts cut off. The product is very popular with kids across the country.

Today, Smucker's holds the top sales in jams, jellies, coffee, cooking oil, and peanut butter. As the company continues to expand, the family keeps growing with it. In May 2016, Timothy's son, Mark, became the president of the company. To this day, Smuckers are still behind their famous family brand, making some of the world's favorite foods!

Timeline

1858	Jerome Monroe Smucker was born on December 5, in Orrville, Ohio.
1891	Willard Smucker was born.
1897	Smucker built a cider mill.
1921	Smucker made his business official and called it the J.M. Smucker Company.
1942	Smucker's products were sold across the United States.
1946	Smucker's paid US government inspectors to review its production.
1948	Smucker died at 89 years old.
1962	Smucker's unveiled its new slogan: "With a name like Smucker's, it has to be good."
1980	Smucker's became the number one brand of jams and jellies on the US market.
2016	Mark Smucker became the president of the company.

Say What?

Smucker's has had several slogans over the years. Many slogans were direct, such as, "Smucker's, the best one . . . the one you're proud to serve." In the 1960s, the company revealed its new slogan: "With a name like Smucker's, it has to be good." What is the meaning behind this slogan?

The Smucker's slogan was meant to refer to the family's unusual last name. The company meant for the slogan to say to customers that since the company had an unusual name, it better serve outstanding products. The Smucker company has since said that the slogan has come to mean something else to its customers. The slogan tells customers that seeing the Smucker's name on a product means the product will be good quality.

Glossary

creamery - a place where butter and cheese are made or where dairy products are prepared and sold.

crock - an earthenware jar or pot.

decade - a ten-year period.

draft - to select for required military service.

economy - the way a nation produces and uses goods, services, and natural resources.

ethics - a set of principles governing an individual or group.

Great Depression - the period from 1929 to 1942 of worldwide economic trouble. There was little buying or selling, and many people could not find work.

instill - to slowly and gradually cause someone or something to feel or have.

legacy - something important or meaningful handed down from previous generations or from the past.

marketing - the process of advertising or promoting an item for sale.

Mennonite - a member of one of the Protestant religious groups founded in Holland in the 1500s. Mennonites are noted for dressing plainly and living simply.

middleman - someone who buys and sells goods. A middleman buys from producers and sells to retailers or consumers.

ration - to control the amount of something people are allowed to have.

share - one of the equal parts into which the ownership of a company is divided.

slogan - a word or a phrase used to express a position, a stand, or a goal.

stock market - a place where stocks and bonds, which represent parts of businesses, are bought and sold.

supervise - to watch over or take care of something.

unique (yoo-NEEK) - being the only one of its kind.

World War II - from 1939 to 1945, fought in Europe, Asia, and Africa. Great Britain, France, the United States, the Soviet Union, and their allies were on one side. Germany, Italy, Japan, and their allies were on the other side.

Websites

To learn more about Food Dudes, visit **abdobooklinks.com**. These links are routinely monitored and updated to provide the most current information available.

Index